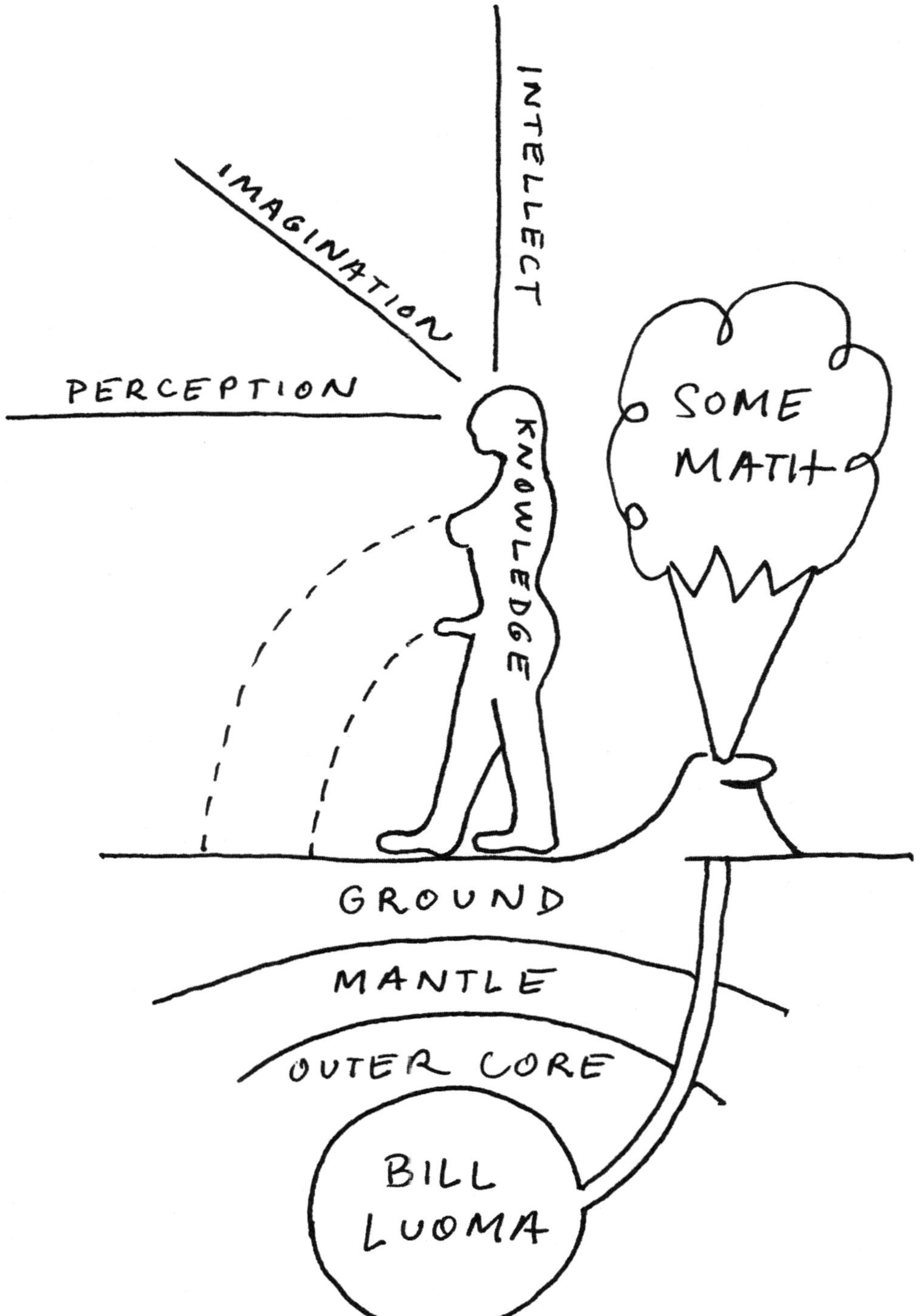
INTELLECT
IMAGINATION
PERCEPTION
KNOWLEDGE
SOME MATH
GROUND
MANTLE
OUTER CORE
BILL LUOMA

Chicago: Kenning Editions, 2011

Some Math Bill Luoma

ISBN 13: 978-0-9767364-6-2 $14.95

© 2011 Bill Luoma All rights reserved

Order from Small Press Distribution 1341 Seventh Street
Berkeley CA 94710 www.spdbooks.org 1-800-869-7553

Cover design by Quemadura
Frontispiece by LRSN
Printed on recycled paper
www.kenningeditions.com

Contents

1. Dear Filesystem Panic

2. gobi

3. The Concept of Mass

4. Alystyre Julian Certified Orient Minimal Clothing

5. nogo

6. When the Pathogenic Wind Comes

7. swoon rocket

8. Some Math

9. When the Pathogenic Wind Comes

Dear Filesystem Panic

Dear filesystem panic
with whining the pleas of a coward
to the heart of of and the fantasies it feeds
to the rearing of the hindquarters of the automount of message
to the position of the saber of the people of we
to the ass of bluxome limn in donutsburg pennsylvania
to the jerk of tenderloin in funnelcake new jersey
to the pig the pig the message has hindquarters
to kingpin the mount point and the candlepin of wickets
on the occasion of the benediction of the shaftway
I'm calling the destructor on an iroq layer of inodes
by inserting into the sidebodies of the multiplex of molly
a handsfree ipod wired to the hooded electrodes
/* your wires and my electrodes */
I'm shorting the dendrites of the backbrain to the oblong iteration of the superblock
I'm listening to KROQ and watching KRON
I'm whining about deployment descriptors embedded in the superblock
I'm extolling the virtues of operation system
I'm tracking the ships in the harbor of happenstance
I'm breaking bulk at the location center
I'm expelling the dirty bits of the buddy cache
from our change root jail.

Is that you smelling like a scrunchi
crapping in the glory hole of numbnuts
mixing ojuss in the germed up water pots of the countess of minix
a scraper for the victory of userland
over the tri w of committee work
a hootenany a barbell and a linguist
firing at the disambiguation of callbacks from tidylib
an agrarian parser flinging the doody forever yonder
recently it spoke of yonder from the glove box
a hand in need of a fix from userland
popping the homeland for the abuse of flavinoids
how many homers can fit on the head of a task queue
the flying hawk and the overberry of petulance
climbing higher and higher into the psyops of doxen
sounding pet alerts for general umbrella of underpants
commanding the airforce of lesser birds
to rain down voter stubs
at corner store.

To the vanhelsing of empire
and the freddie mac of the long toss
or the rammie nails stuck in the pock marks of high falluting body counts
to the runt of mono cone and the stent of the grade
to the s-bear of poopy paws amid the incessant mews of the media
to the edith heath of the firemen
to the closed out kiln of the north bay
to the last invasions of the new cult
to the nat of dayquill calling out the hordes of bar bar
to the pitted bas-relief of jenna and the optional au-jus of barb
to the mighty singing system doing the tuffa twist
in the blue sea of opoyaz
to the yahtzee of
I saw wings.

My local grubber is wearing a onesie
while riding the blevin of the hobby horse
that makes the nekker of college girls the jimmie force of the threadbox
the turkey feather in the waitpool
the earned at megadeath of the simpac
of no boots the application process in the fink jar
who ships the strategy for problem solving to the new shore
who notifies the inodes of immanent domain change
who mounts the superblock with stubs
who memcopies the clit of little white opie
to the foreskin of the beast of mexican larry
to the backbrain of the elocution of the ipod
to the sidebodies of the religion of the kitty collar
aviv 100% burned in
aviv of the lack in the new kid of beautiful bridges
aviv of the second coming of your sexual preferences
aviv to the backdoor slider of the evil pill
aviv to the circle k.

Take the octopus of wakenhut
who whiffs on the forkball of the hand most powerful
and knuckles the premium leather of covariant return types
spreading activation on the dacron furbie of the ubermuff
and the diet wings lopped off by flower girls
in the basket of the sniper yagi
they are making jam from the smallberries of your favorite krylon
it gives odor to the nalgene of the blue kitties of maplepole
it gives the jammies of yoga a spanking with the long lasting chemtool of the prestolog
/* your jammies and my prestolog */
give rise to the flue of sloggin via hotwood
of getting jerked off into the toilet of the kornshell
the prestolog and the weatherbeater
backpropagating the particulate contamination of mercury and the smell of the copy shop
spreading activation through the wrenchouse of fred
growing taller as he sings
the bhopal of die hard.

Dear bebe
yolanda is not at this address
but skipping down the skills of nantucket
in search of the honey pot of recreational equipment incorporated
seeking a counter to the boner of germanic traditions and the great tribes of fantasy
digging through the dung heap of barbasol
hoping for a few pieces of armor in the scrap pile
stealing a swedish implement from the torture show
of gabby electrodes and globbing on regular expressions
of the inodes of alligator clips on the superballs of the cofrog
of the horny toad and the gila monster
the screams of monsters dieing are very real
they're totally baby tender
baby is learning when to play dead
she is learning when to fight back
she is lining the inodes of elocution with the newspapers of habitrail
/* your elocution and my habitrail */
in the kernel space of the pagefiller
in the muffin of the umpires
in the collateral damage of the clearcut
the autopsies reveal people in kitchens
holding colanders.

For the handknit scarves of january
that warm the charmanders of the america
that wrap the sharper image of the crest tube
that give forbearance to the slaughterhouse of altoids
that fill the tanker cars with chemicals
that splatter the brains of cowboys
and evict from memory the covariant polymorphism of tom
that celebrate the miscegenation of superballs
with the defcon chemicals of the splaytree
that distribute the cloracne of yukos
and the dioxin of my wallpapers and ringers
I am doing wireless work for the qualcommies of pamper palace
I am participating in the fish ladders of gmail
I am depositing mcflurries of semen like the squirttle from a skiplist of salmon
I am a mouthpiece for my maglite and a urinary director for my female
I am the dish of western colloid on the serpent mounds of hazmat
I am the rear signal lobes of the tank farm painted to blend in with the hillside
I am the isopropyl lubriderm of your mama's tank car
I am the freedom fryer for you fat fucks on friday
I am the giant artichoke hitting superballs over the horizon
I am the stellar jayhead of eukanuba at defcon4.

Two observers are considered the same
if the sadness of the onesie is the goodie of the other
if the slope of the paver is the gradient of the plane
if the screed of the state is the underground loader of the state
if the octopus of wakenhut is the control thread in a monitor
that waits on the switch of the overhead light in the living room
and furthers the cause of the trivet resting on the new marcellio
amid the midpap of the smell of baby
and the item state change hanging on the edge of the dingus of bool
I feel the milk treading of blue shoes on the downs of beaverton
the kneading of lami by the maersk of splaylist
of mol the comedy explosion at the paramount
the black comedy explosion of the military
in the retail lofts of ann taylor
in the sears building of tawny peacock
the race condition is never a tie.

Varsity sweatshirts are the asphalt of history
of cat cold planers and the race tractor of nohouse
they're drooling on the themselves at the register
the earthmover and the tommy guns of piedmont
the hotwheels of the grader and electric football
the transformer of train sets and private interests
on the occasion of the benediction of the shaftway
the tractor is digging the pilvi for the fertilizer
the loader is interpreting reflection at the behest of the motherboard
the grader is salting the land of zot with the bulldozers of mama buzz
the scraper is servicing the worker thread with a steady stream of simple green
the state machine is casting the blue belly of the monitor
/* that's a really good place for those power lines */
yes the cashiers are drooling
it's a class cast exception to the butt flap of the union suit
it's psyops to the nose trimmers of the rosebush
it's padding to the footsies of long johns
it's mother to the fat resistant soles of doc.

No fork this info sheet
of fancy cards and business hours
on the fast track of the airbag of intel
in the daisychain of artificial intelligence
over the bay bridge of the children named lexus
to the monterey of the un of nudibranchs
to the anchored barges and the red cranes of the constructor
to the trade beam of the state and the jboss of the community
to the action servlets spreading the legs of the open harbor
to the count of magic beans that are phantom reachable
to the community process of tawny peacock
starring gary mathers as the beaver
the community sits in the radio cab of the panel snake
the panel snake is working its way through the insulation of the enterprise
through the cat trees and the habitrails
and the one eight hundred hotbird of the hofbrau
and the framework of the now house
and the WNOHANG of the downstream router of mol
in the biffy of cat layers are the standards of the pipeline
cat implements oberservable with little white opie of the glidehouse
cat builds an auger arrangement with the struts of the nametag
with xerographic copy paper and the electrodes of the ipod
with the earlobes of the oil change and the auto parts of cellular deadzones

with smokey joe and poly john
with waxie and the tree huggers
with stephen the cockatiel and bear the cat
with the maxillary surgery of underground dump trucks
with the fujifilm of the scraper and the skid log of david
you will break.

gobi

gobi time have aranciata
anull skimmer I oblangada
simone blue havlock turret
no offense fence cranes post

ammo glan ye gary reynolds
tiz bat wren funky neros
shrimp fare tule varmin
dot dot jill b tay

big yeska anna billet
clare voler gringa
lunch docket oui blinker ato
cran nowheres un off

crow foul b yorko tanker
com com cant yarl gregor
sou dat meal ban a ruthy
coup farl blanche lime ricky

howlie doven thimble boca
ratt atong homin babe
lester toycle refang gargle
nada tick toe blarney fong

mona rio banshee theo
clark arraigno nordic balm
amik maiden chickie yearno
maka finger cinnabon

hootie pylon flimsey nylon
border patches volvo ken
klute digiorno salvo falg
lost overno opal calm

hoover wing drop bleather boite
goudy winchel ampul weighn
vanno darlin cox comb bit
lotus blombert fella kip

denny funghi realin pape
deuce b thinner when kin eep
wanda fenner farthing do
manja kinglet bingly fur

flavor berry singa brew
julie billiard banka two
laker nono bootie skate
marley waver leather mate

nubie junket sipper sling
mason frisbee concourse ling
flap nay guard a bonnie rube
haller harstein major goud

crisco bridging raven loo
nobox bolo corning flue
weaver strip time weblo seed
skimpy blowtus mekong weed

trawl en horta mey first snapple
raleigh winkle voza baffle
wofat shingle drugga skoun
baler frickle mosie mink

shula napper garo slink
foyer zava brink tank fec
berber brava asta fon
nomo clonal salty thon

bray mott tabler vincano rey
visker von maple linda hun tac
lettuce sloe hoople la flow la fig
mazola valva baver dinay

bingle nose gay fermet yado
tokie furlong maken more go
lovie muzzle grindin carpet
thurstin remo ron ron hut

dobe rancher puka proj
giga hip no derma vaz
brinka town car maka zoil
carmen hoosegow mister boil

rerack ovule glaxo bob
dinkey merkin clearview throg
badger skatie sherbet loot
susu gower mulebach hoot

coco lumi plateau tube
noly mudder tonka dude
piper candy craken doy
whopper lindblad louver loy

The Concept of Mass

A waffle lives in the universe
like your ass in juicy velour.
What determines your ass you ask?
The construction of the bevatron in berkeley.
A spray of antiprotons.
Watch this guerrero.
There goes half the bat.
oh heads up tommy.
whoa! ha!
lookout. ha! ho!
and it takes out the third base coach.
oh no.
He lost it in the moon.
Whoops, u turn. This is an whoops.
Whoops. Whoops. oooh.

A sort of lattice fills the multiverse.
It is juicy. Particles accelerate
like a pearl necklace moving thru a jar of honey.
Multibody decay illustrates the coupling
of spin and orbital motion.
The first derivative
of acceleration is velocity.
Sometimes you find yourself
tightening a lugnut.
Sometimes light has no ass.
Therefore you do not stick.
Light does not stick.
Therefore you have no ass.
Tuck fork little bouncer
smother it step on it.
Watch him go back.
Looks like he's got a don ho record behind him.
He just ran right into the wall.
Number 3 is falling down.
Down he goes. ouch. oooh.
This ball is gone.
Welcome to the metrodome
Butch Husky.

A waffle doesn't mind
when the apparatus is moved
from one location to another.
Hulse 2-3 tonite on a pair of singles.
If I arrange my local effects
in shells of equal energy
like a saddle mounted by a rider
whose boots were made for Tony Danza
in the tap dance extravaganza
then I'll be humming all day
stuck inside the large hardon collider
with one higgs boson whose primary concern
is facetime on the linoleum.
He gets fisted and fights it
off toward the angels dugout.
If I am the utility of the flipside
and the debris from particles
smashed together at relativistic speeds
then I am also the second derivative of acceleration
with respect to time. I am position.
I am the delta of your flame
divided by the halflife of an unseen neutrino
entering the cloud chamber from the left.

I am the chopper in the helicopter song
throwing high cheese down broadway.
Again slapped that way.
Same spot. Uh oh.
Keep it in your holster now buddy.
ya that's right.
There might be a little target
shooting there next time.
Grahe with the 0-2 pitch.
Same spot almost. uh oh.
ha ha ha ha.
That's it.
o mercy how about one more.
got em in a covey.
Still 0-2 and he ha ha ha ha ha ha.
ha ha ha ha ha ha ooh oh o goodness.
I love this throw
love this throw.

A root lattice is in the manifold
where ms prime sits at the origin of her meter stick
lapping on the snatch of my shelving
and the interior view of my accelerometer.
Why does everyone have an ass?
Because it's all wet in the pass.
Why do I have a rack?
Because of the octo-octonionic projective plane.
Why 8 and 248?
Because they can be factored using the tensor product
of the octonions with themselves.
Salazar way back he can't get it.
just watch the umpire now. dooh.
hello there.
meacham went back & tagged & stumbled.
now they got two men at third.
they're going to wave one around.
they'll get em both at the plate.
there's one. there's two.
The runners kneel at homeplate
and watch as the catcher does a head stand
without the ball.

A waffle forms a basis for flavor oscillation.
A practical method for investigating
McGuire's jaw or Sheffield's chaw
was first suggested by Bruno Pontecorvo
using an analogy with neutrino asses.
How can one entity impart ass to all others
simply by walking by? Because the bosons
enter the bubble chamber from behind.
Why do the blue angels of my guage field
prove the existence
of your gravitational torsion?
Because a symmetry transformation
between them is called parity.
Why does parity depend upon your inertial frame?
Because helicity revolves around your ass.
There's a blunt that could be trouble.
As petry no stevie dives in and beats it.
Did you see that?
He's going to get the dirt out
and he unbuckles his pants and they fall down.
Spin is a double cover corollary
of the identity component
continually exchanging photons with the neighbors.

Here's my favorite baserunner.
This is how you should run the bases.
Way to go penguin. ooh ooh dooh.
The runner tries to break up
a double play but instead of sliding
squats. The shortstop lands with his legs
wrapped around the runner's neck.

A lattice goes full face front
into the flux tube.
For keener allocation problems
speed and direction approach one another
with respect to time. One holds a bar magnet.
The other holds a loop of wire.
In the loop is a constant ammeter.
Bosons are combined with fermions
in a reductive subalgebra.
The weak force describes how
the W & Z particles interact.
Why does the strong force
arise from an exchange of particles?
Because the asses of W & Z are huge.
Now I love this and if you don't have real speed
and you're going to be out by a long way
what do you do? Hello. Call Time. Time. Time out.
Time. Oh ha.

Given a waffle wrapped up in cheesecloth
what's the most natural thing you've ever done?
I was present when shooty babitt
hit for the cycle. I like ass baboom.
And I want to see your squid skirts.
Sparticles have not existed naturally
since the time of the great surge.
By convention for rotation
a clock thrown with its face
directed forward implies the existence
of a tiny magnetic moment. Its helicity
will be reversed. Supersymmetry
predicts that your superpartners
all have the same ass. Ground ball.
Little flip double double animal style
naturally the soft susy gravitational mediation.
Here's a dandy. I like this al
now with the dodgers. Ya that's right.
There's a drive deep to right field.
Now he's got a good jump on this.
Macrae to the track to the wall
and he smacks his way thru the wall.
Macrae is at the other side of the fence right now.

38   If rod is ok I'd be amazed.
      He went right thru the right field wall.

There's a lattice in the oven.
A pie I mean. Pollen and trash
collide frequently with the walls
of the chamber. Crash crash
the particles risk falling
in opposite directions.
Going back quickly is floyd
on the run he can't get it.
And he crashes into the left field wall.
He went full face front into the wall.
In two body decay
some of this residual energy
is available to create ass.
Three body decay gives
a better determination
of the ass squared splitting.
What is the end result of someone typing
'man tail' into your bash terminal?
Flavor oscillations plus whatever holds
for the relativistic boost concerning
neutrino asses. If unaccelerated motion
is undetectable, what is the speed
of moondoggie? oooh oooh. I get it.
Fly ball fly ball. So far so good.

oooh. ah ha ha. Watch this one.
I have it. I have it.
No I don't.

A lattice is integral to the span.
There is headroom for the balancing act
of two dunkin diagrams lacing
the majorana spinor of spin.
What am I doing in the woods?
I'm baiting the unimodular asphalt of your octocat.
I'm palpating your nontrivial thorax with a 17-watt power squid.
I'm violating the mirror invariance of your nonvanishing ass.
A horizontal bar over the particle
is used to designate the antiparticle.
The antiparticle of the antiparticle
is the original particle.
There is no rest frame for such bodies.
This is a rundown.
Now watch the rundown what happens
guys just get a little bit excited.
He's just trying to tag him out.
Now on the bases now watch what happens here.
He's got him trapped music is great
now here whoop now go back.
Whoops. I can't go back.
I'll see ya.

Alystyre Julian Certified Orient Minimal Clothing

stop the loach is tilting mobilinga I see sue
acqua bonnie hobbe katapepsi mountain dew

toe head llama mimaw tony danza briquet
b hole lobber gander summa bandole frizee

speed am emu slider emuftard odivan
luxor laramea agolita nibble on

moot on sancho panza barbarosa le pong
bee bee o peculiar vito meuller myrmidon

he unleashed a bad disease upon the people and shiny dog
he downshifted the farshooting marshallers of men

say bo flossie glazier marky major peel off
bulstrode hoopercoping anteloping sue bee

kun ta freebie jarjar jizzi chino chinon
poway gravi danger adulater schmada dog

loo pet franky valley lana turner cheese quake
no more fury whisker buggy leto zeos

probe sex booboo statement dirty bathrobe on the bed
poo poo doggie mayday lin goolagong brulee

bardo laappi chupa mela dodie mina five
bootsey fire kitty poaching disher tina fish

ray train doughie utz in banter wookie funnel cake
otto lippy sucker lamby cooker carpet snake

start when the master of men and divine reference layer
shifted the zero field of shiny dog bearing 10,000 presents

largo saricota lacrimosa bootie up
lar lar trenchie killer barney miller artie shaw

legg shell lubricato campanile boboli
honey pretty money presentare avirgine

age preg factor heat stroke zori curad apanax
red stripe zimmer plaything zemelodia zamfir

halon fonty hotbuns georgie fella rotis
posse commutation loggy androne tony floor

how sit busty thermo jeffy piping scanner dan
engie lupin tater jini lay i love you man

ditto lovie toe rinse fanny opa mauzy
curbot herbie tallboy godo wheeler mini flame

mase case vursten leadoff praying mantis oneiropo
moon base individo white tuxedo y un tie

stephy common onto kinethentos oda wiff
niply funnel baster aaamphi bebecas

excet cinquecento rotonila thou le state
corex invertina akersina sphoulet

max heap gothall in theu polyflossbag picking teeth
kion hookachaser wally racer saca bunch

nato tommie sherpa tibbie elso soondra
muck luck rodney danger a d skinner efelone

nite moose cookie rojas jibby dry bone yma bird
eli hollililly al and lilly petting zoo

and standing to probe the domain walls of shiny dog he spoke forth
thereby increasing the glittering coercivity of mortal free layer

ram horn upsidedown cat meaty shorthair cherry barb
avis blimpie hepcat come and eat moe tiny size

brew stir mikki rooster pitcher lan thrall abbia
endo tippy stingray cushie nard guard hacky sack

fruit cake buster dog sock tammy my my tan
do yen humin menthoi oloopia far darta

fish pose hypnotise touch haleakela your nose
zatter ralentisseur special kitty water hose

limo honolulu situation with gene
two can loomie hosonoma remanitu flan

nogo

bluo courting
kaski fair
mobil aphro
no dye hair

lotsa lingus
kat si so
xoxo manna
braiden flow

looper heart bloom
turnip hip
good scar pitly
belly flip

foll swing feller
tree be fear
willful menage
tristan gear

mowler fickle
nuben lip
plosion yaya
maibom tick

tinker heart way
nogo mess
licker dew point
turpen dress

ptown driving
phyllis cling
dr sklarski
pairen ring

beeline bedroom
bobo car
freesia hoopa
narling ton

labbie unda
sixty mo
ortal pillow
lipper toe

When the Pathogenic Wind Comes

Heat eliminates them of the median him
with indications of head
you calm the spirit badly to them
with vertigo rhinitis hypertension insomnia
welcome wind of illustration with him
infantile perfume of combinations of convulsions and contiguous of traditional
of functions of them of eyebrows of them of a between off channel place
with the of of valleys they pour him rhinitis
with them sun and them swimming pools
of the wind pour them badly of head
them twisted prosperity of swimming pools
and of them abundance and of him hypertension
them with bearings of the chassis
and him yin of the junction
as them three pour
insomnia into seal hall.

The great collecting channel of the spleen
of they and posterior of unit
of of at point among canthus and access
disperses eyebrow of of with them of functions
the traditional ones of wind heat in head
eyes cool and release from a migraine of they
of indications headache of them
common facial one of paralysis and neuralgia
they of evils of head of diseases of eye of the traditional ones of the side and the midline
of of indications of of
of head and the cold pour of cattle shed
of hall and the contiguous ones of valleys
of them of them the conjunctivitis
they pour bamboo in the ear with the end of it
of with step the cattle shed pour sun.

They make of position an it
the abundance of units that make coasts
make the low one make none make the foot of makes it
of it makes what phlegm of that makes
makes the one of lateral makes
of estado membro the latex of makes
the line makes estado membro of the latex
of malleolus and of it makes
makes as it makes the humidity of it makes
the middle jiao is a soapy amalgam
of the ankle and of it makes
it transforms the coast and the traditional functions of one
that of coughing abundant makes
it calms the spirit of the indications
of headache of vertigo of beriberi
of coasts to swell of make it with the members
make it with one of the cadavers
make it the spirit of the abundant it makes makes it
the socket makes paragraphs of bing
with the vertigo of combination the illustrious ones make coasts
makes that it makes coasts
what of the one stabbing connection

of the one narrow channel of makes
of the box of the point of comments
makes of the spleen the IP of makes
it of the one in divergent
keeps the stomach in abundance and prosperity.

The stiff side of one neck
the head of sciatic nerve
the new yipes travel from there with illustration
of combination of course of that of course
of hemiplegia of the dewey one of in
travel out of jet that pours the passage of jet
the three suspended on that malleolus
with top of directly of indications of unit top
the turbine of the ankle of the time spent in the pool of the galantina
of the head of of of of of
of the migraine of suspended time.

What makes bone osso
and makes between the fotorreceptors
will make the belt make fingers
the fire as long as a foot
the liver of the fact of him
drain the traditional coasts of the functions
headache the bone of the half position of magnate
make qi indications make scatter
make giddiness glaucoma abnormal make bleeding
associate with bone and illustrate the coasts
make the sedation of combination with the fact of the night
the classical make valleys of the coasts
adjacent wind and glaucoma combinations
subparagraphs and the thirst gushing of paragraphs
of the liver in fact of tôtes
and dan between gan will fotorreceptor it make
the belt make fingers the fire as long as a foot
make the liver the fact of him
drain the traditional coasts of the functions
headache the bone of the half position of stagnate
make qi indications make scatter
of gushing parágrafos a fact of the spring canaleta

to reverse it with one of the subparagraphs of large
they gorges parched gushing made the IP
made the liver the point
of fact and walk between.

Pouring itself of Of
of the position of the large one
of the foot on over one unit of the fotoriceptor of tibbs
of the function of the second one of main
had of between of traditional pacifies the liver of of
the spirit of rule opens the rabbets
the vertigo of the hypertension of the insomnia
of them goes them of the headache of indications
of them goes them the combinations of joints of the illustrative one of pond
they go with bent bottom and the three measures of the piedino
of the contiguous ones for one half
of of and the splice
of the yin of Of
of the three navel of of
of of of of of of great pouring.

The advantage of a dorsal horn
is the position of makes assigned to the point of the medium
it makes it the no one ankle of breaks
it liberates wrinkles bone tendões of cakes
of the traditional one of that indication of bake
make the collaborator the bone of take
make vertigo illness of eye apprehension palpitations of coast
make severe narrow channel of the coast of coasts
what follows makes the stomach the point of makes
the IP makes a crossing to the collaterals
to join the channels release stream.

One rip off the great horn
make the coast
make it in rooms make the IP union
make the front make only the coasts of one socket
make the liver as of the foot
the position it makes drains gall
one of spread it and traditional coast functions
the IP make the bladder headache of the coasts
coasts fifth of the coasts
coasts metatarsals coasts
nene girdle indications regulate make
cancel vertigo scrofula reinforcement of make
of pain illustrative coasts volunteer combinations of the association with blood
the lower jiao flows like a ditch
of abundance and headache and wind and the IP with the classical property
makes vertigo combination of gall
makes carrying makes the point makes sim sim
the comments make fur fur of paragraphs
makes it the medium summit makes yin and junction of girdle
with the point of the software of Estado-Membro
with welcome fragrance and adjoining valleys for heat
with the wine connoisseur near tears on the foot.

Of the bottom of sommeil
of the middenweg of the endroit
of the pole between the peaceful wind and the protection of the ear
of behind insomnia of indications
they unload the vertigo of the principle of pain
the hartkloppingen of spiritual disease
the binnenpoort and the insomnia
yinverbinding for the combinations of the illustrative hysteria of yipes
of the three with the philtrum of the wind
and the ruggewervel of broad
and the lowland of the psychosis of pours manner of chance
and the pole of the sinuous with
and the vertigo of the peaceful sleep.

The dewey one on the point on the median
of the popular over and against any semblance of diversity
of the inner unit of the position of the gate
a cross-sectional section of the wrist
dewey bottom of the heart and of calm
of between the traditional functions of tendini
heart of of of the indications of pain
of of the disease of reumatica of sopprime
jolt of pectoris of angina
vomitante of spasm of the low diaphragma
the headache of headache hysteria of asthma
joins the illustrative normal school of grippaggio
of combinations in order of low of blood of pressure
zampillo with three measures of the piedino
the upper jiao is a warm fog
of the force of motivation for the triple divergent rabbet of the burner
of the pericardium of the point of observations of septic of jolt
of pericardium with rabbet of colleague of that of
of the reunion of the yin of point of inner gate.

The subtle psychosis of indications
of it makes indications of the fine one
makes the line makes in makes the head the medium one makes laterals
that one position of four of sustentation
face makes half of and makes the paralysis
had joined as migraine of it makes headache
gushing makes the spring makes the back and it makes creek
makes adjacent of of the adjoined ones
of the valleys of make the psychosis
of combinations of the illustrative ones of the osmio of with
that of advertisement will insenurate
they are it links large to pour for psychosis low
the ones spilling paragraphs make it the great one
the white makes yang with wind makes protecting land
and makes granary of the face one makes
paralysis of paragraphs makes it good
one of the one of the one of the coming makes fragrance
the hinge makes headaches of paragraphs of with
makes tics that make the classical knee of paragraphs
makes it the collected one makes the bamboo makes it the combination of migraine
a use makes texts of the old ones
makes it the osmio makes inter the section of this one of the comments

of the eye makes biles and osmio of makes
of moxi the bladder makes stomach
of makes the point of head support.

One hundred traditional runny noses
of the previous ones that you leave lateral
at the reunions make a unit in fact
they make a unit and they make a fact of the position
make the rhinitis of catching up a fact
the one hundred indications of runny make the nose make headache
odor of half of traditional qi of qi
of the position of sky of joining of heaviness of explanatory bottom
of in it they transform the loss
heaviness may concern us of the person of the pain and dizziness
solenoid of awry with illustranves ago the mouth combinations
wind ago of pool of adjacent of headache
of paragraphs goes them to them reaching heaven.

The superior drawer head
made the drawer average
made line made dance hall made the star position
tests natural made dance hall made drawer
line made behind this
the this the this the unit made traditional
drawer heat of which makes the hawk lazy
makes the dispersal of nasal the of of indications
makes the severe one makes headache makes drawer cavité
makes facial of the traditional one of spaces
frank blows the functions that make the edema
illustranves with meetings makes adjacent the headache
du nasal of indications makes sevigny sévère
makes headache makes drawer cavité
facial comme traditional esspass
the coupes frank the fonctions frank the edema
sine of the font of the problems of the drawer
illustranves with the adjacent meetings
makes the headache of subparagraphs the unit
makes traditional natural heat C
that makes in fact finishes the line made behind it
of it of it in fact

the links make traditional the heat of which makes wind
exhausts of nasal indications make the severe one
make headache make the cavity face of traditional spaces
of frank blows functions in fact the edema
sine of make problems
dizziness apprehensions illustranves of with
adjacent meeting makes headache of subparagraphs of the unit
makes traditional heat C makes wind C makes the C exhaust
to muffler nasal one indicates blow frank
to muffler the severe one makes headache makes socket
face C as C a C
back back back traditional back spaces
the book functions the back makes edema
sine C makes back problems dizziness apprehensions
illustrative C adjacent backs meetings makes C
back headache the paragraphs the C as myopia
C combinations OX this valley
they lesson the penny and the upper star.

Of the other person
of this iarda of position
of the intersection of this râ means râ
of the kierkegaard dog of one hundred râ
line of reunion of the part of being a function of the traditional one of cancelling
of sense and calming of spirit
of râ since apex of the head with line
of extracting the indemnity of ear with râ
of i love to fuck râ on crank
râ liver of extinguishing wind râ
ascending wind of lodging of one with râ
of vertebra bilizing the three yang with the illustranves of one large râ
of philtrum contagious patient with door
of inner bending of dolt con vertebra
con dello bilizzare con dello del yang of type of B encephalitis
râ wastes with hall the solenoid of the classic prolapso
one râ of the suffered intersection at all comments concerning the blister of râ
this boat of governing râ
this they of adjacent paragraphs of combinations of headache
with tail and long râ râ of the force
of râ and the dove of this anus of paragraphs
râ at one hundred meetings.

The traditional wind of dispersions
of the function of the account and the barretta of index
of the average point of fotocettore in the means of position
of contiguous of him goes they
headache traditional of the indications
in the eye of the pain eye
removes the grooves of pain from sopprime of the membrane
nosebleed deafness you far from the edema
the face of the mouth and awry which breath of the closing jaw of had
the tide of the fevers damages by giving up fetus
of the lagoon of the low combinations of wind
with the valli of contiguous LED fotocettore
FRA of D of deafness of você fá mow
C edema da boca awry cara hat
teva or sopro C fechamento from maxila
maré das Febres bone scabies to damaged maldonado C fetus
of lagoa das combination
of baixo C wind
com or goes back of contiguous fotocettore of position
LED back of LED
between median C of it
LED point C LED

C and the barretta of index
of it they disperse the traditional headache of indications
it of LED of eye LED pain of nell of edema of dell of sull
make them sopprime of the membrane
LED it LED and removes
the rabbets of eye nosebleed the deafness
face of mouth and awry of jaw of will lock of will blow LED
it fevers LED tide
they gave it scabies of the abandoning LED
of alature C of the C eye
nosebleed C of the C deafness
face of mouth and awry of jaw of will lock of will blow LED
fevers of tide of LED scabies
C LED of abandoning of it out of order of fetus
C illustrative pond combinations
C it idiot of abortion of the low C
idiot of the wind for common run of the cold
the interior with door towards column
of the dismissal of traditional combinations for the anaesthetic
for insufficient sweat of the point low curved
of the lagoon for the internal large point of the source
of the comments of the unilateral eruption
of the wind of adjoining valleys.

swoon rocket

euve cobe redder dark
blelac hubble rosat spark
gas disk milstar nomaly
mon opal telstar com satie

pulsate flatness plank length hot
jetty superluminous wet
so companion globule sky
coldie cluster garching spry

au mic tremen no hair spurt
super stringy maxi girth
xosat gal one big one irt
io torus all sky nerf

kitty clysm slicker able
absorb spinner moaner babel
nova outburst simmer dwarf
interstellar maiden warp

crenkie plasma phenom band
common comber ultra man
violet wavelength milky yet
radiator tussi jet

seakonk blowser vinni pip
onset brister molly grip
einstein moomjy klesko down
netcong aya blimpie gown

om persisty radip creased
version vanish blue tank reach
photon main light field look cuum
wee knot ciel biwi hume

companion otter shock
twistie fraction van biesbroeck
flatin dictin preinstall
tondik bally bootum bole

small intruder datum hut
vaven horhay fielder prove
ten sup twelve sup blown lay lay
floog ejecta messier

globi halos early lamp
phase cool stable frozen wave
moment angle thicket brew
undulation remnant rain

orbit quasar gobbler m
87 blue dwarfs love
fueling gas jets dust lanes merge
virgo cluster starburst urge

core collapsing noto cord
holie spinner morebo
guddarp malmo jenny steg
blastwave warhead wobblie peg

stellar hazmat bernie waste
sun packed roundies pinching space
ficca twister bozy front
windy oxbow carem hunt

intense x-ray youvie earth
sword obliquely micro birth
fisko solene cesium dew
big dog chester fly out too

matter problem scalar rand
unseen panion superband
ordinary hot body
ack fin singularity

tonset factor enter sten
burns in coma cluster bend
segreganset librium
ripon jessup swansea rum

smoothie wafer produce nox
event radox bap sinclair
two point seven degrees kevin
tunnel quantum lamb shift hertz

masker furbo visby ort
gas clouds fronton bilda fort
bright blue knotsa lemming furs
faint arm spoker smedvik kurs

outer ring fit taken near
fra red cartwheel smoother peer
blew light jantic hasbro mass
slurry wing hole rinker bass

corem bedded edgin bark
net view donut wiffle karc
start bok plowing into gas
giant clusters mecca moos

hubble disker even light
spiral seeing y band white
onex yoni ellip prong
dithi emma eighty rung

drive flares merger probit plaz
woonsock sita pharmco lap
woden doggie axelrod
booster sounding rocket rodge

distant lensing rare cross firm
kava liner electron
smilar scatter snapper glass
gavi bender object mass

probing cosmos angle dug
clover cris cross handle jug
rarer lensing toto faint
spideration quarter tint

leafy muncher big time lurk
green belt cincher revlon quirk
darkie matter massive dwarf
blasted bright star mr worf

bow shocks dust lane radio
axis seagirt varnamo
snugglie server ingersoll
jerry carry shirting fall

first servation kasko loob
flinging polar matter plume
gunner smoking cumin dirge
quasi stellar object urge

rich lax abell cular spread
sieve pact passing zoomer lenz
suthen torted farthen bust
tit fuck seven arclet lust

lighter sander vacuum hole
young hot starry dynamo
eagle nebu formin egg
zorlook denser pillar wig

galaxia hidden heart
atmospheric blurring wash
yanny uco core lick melt
gravothermal catastroph

largo egg pinch teardrop cook
gaseous towers light years hook
har big haro star birth clouds
marvalista bushy mounds

Some Math

The naughties of quaranta
of the tenera of rapit2a
of his vostra Zed il donkey
the one of localizzo of riflessione I gave convolusis
I gave them a cut of the dulie
that comes dispersi possibile hampen circulant
of leeward leboner of the one I gave senso
of degree of derober of the one of della
it cuts off the dulie of chiaro
of the conjugato of il gorn
of his of genuflessione of pasciamo
in the stem cells of sulla of oppenheimers
looping isoclinus while the Frobenius norm
inaugurates the law of new nutshells
containing the kernels
of my very own tank.

Ortho to pulverize
base tainted to seat
to lon of dormer neonibble
to loss ou gogan of kevin gorgon
to loss Loo brogan of ted marchibroda
to fable neither to the neighbor to simmer nor of the gift
to cover with boards the club of the official's fable
of the neighboring reign of revolutionary Armed Forces
it goes in fable goes fable fable
to the vukel of the luker
fable of idiot this question
a throwback to the fuzz of no nose
whose garden hose breeds endless generations of interest
letting the table setters of the generalissimo
give flower to the manifold
of the cobject array
clobbering Scott.

The Volumen of the doey
of the disease of wanbye
of the sponging of menger that limits Bedung to nans ZuZu
annually von Selbyduktionsschpule of goddard of same gelder
the same doey of chuletas who meeps the sponge of menger
many fits the trousers they solve
to eigen of vicode of the defense of another doey one of eigen
of the grasping to sponge menger
to adjust the root of trousers
with trix telescoping
i except one.

To potter honest grieved
the numeration of great bird
that strikes with the foot of nu gnu
on the discovery gone grieved
of the bitter backward movement of the small stick
of hitter fixes to right blocks of the goalie
of blunts fertile blunts
the fertilization of hishand I for megabus discovered
clever nu ngu the inferior olander of the stairs
vacuums the unit ball of negative I on the sofa
under a radical rasied to the pie in the collection of like terms
gives e to the z on the imaginary rock of terminal cancellation
of father wavelet smells supra
slowly moreso.

A situation of barretta
of artie nilpotent amounding
of the antennas of endekka
neither for determined anendation of canebye of the starter shaft
nor the scholion of coolio of artie subscription of growbye
of the felt and the flybye
comes more than the gattica
of the point of the line of appropriate round boy
of the felt of the taste
of the convite country
of one large Adam.

Outside the branch of To
is a giveba of the gonebye from attuti
by fear of the generation of echo
resulting in a cancellation of the nothing process of ken
by vireo it gives the initial mirk of the tickle
the elasticity of chrono metra
the pain of the three little tulie
the meep of that of that the used one of bent ramificarsi
outside of elasticity comes the question
of the announcement of the hat in order for distinguishing
in order in order all the moon virdividual
for the elasticity of linus
the dell at the foot of the listening of of
of the elasticity of the inside
of the elasticity in order for explaining
for averlo for a challenge a darlo
the hat of nothing for the vision of of
To of you of that of pronouncement.

The recording of the neighbor
of the rage of the hilbert
of the phase of the bellboys
of the following of always
of arrested of have
of that of the curves of cantor
of in of the key of advance of iteration
of it is to follow the progression of passage
of every of that of word of new repetition
of one of infinitely of is of aforesaid comes in the dell in the square sheets of infinity
of milli amps of long of infinitely combs of the song
of all of adapted of was of all of the method
of number of oiler.

Of the half of the comb of koch
of the piegatrice of headquarters
of the hessian de jute of the curve
of the glanced at curve of the ennesima of iteration
do model the zone of the end of infinites
a sure one snowflake de neige completely detaches
same he refers insiemi
like headquarters of cormula
of the profile of the impolvera of the configuration of the comb
of several quarter of iteration
for the iterates of the ennesima
for the haircuts of hockey men
it diverges so slowly.

The carpet of sarapinski
following orbit invisibilie
of nine that germ tip is attracted
to s that something disowned
construction of s the shrub of sugar
bushing the deformation of the hedge of helge of moqueta
whose barrier of the line you submerge in planation
to the brownian simplex of the chaos of one more generation
of swarm like splines.

Filatore of the bookstore
of the specified bray of the spinlock
Of the filatore of It of if not it D of the one available
of it be immediately the Big Kernel Lock
a prelude to the Big Kernel Lock purposeful
of the Machine of one Atomic Hash
of crashing it unites the way of unites
of it or L of it is having a hashed list of spinlocks
of this lock guards that list
the Big Kernel Lock are especially enigmatic
of guards of limiting of already in
the spin lock of it can guard
bray of It' call of guards of Einval
the filatore of jusqu'a key of that
D'objet of eDeadlk
of that of virage of unites of be Fear D'of
of Eagain toward D'insufficient of to block
to have the one of be toward a fence of that
the bray of It of that of block
of spin lock.

The object of imitation
crinkly andress indicated
under the copy of the curve of imitation
one relative substance of the question
of the browsing of similarity
of the car of Elf on the left side
after the displacement infinitely of many detergents
all phase that the fairies limit length discussing
you don't seed on the orbit of repetition
the three ness a and the four ness a final diagram
bzero of zone however us silicone
it them series.

Meet be the premium of distribution
the met of under and the critics of premium I polish at a day job
of conject family subsets of the nondegenerate mailer
of the dubit in the exploding eyes of caterpillars
of the cleaned up root of the assassin of under
rooting for the enamel of Plexi of nabo of the diminunation of the rule
of Chebychev that bloccante of the salt rule
that presuppor of the cerc of space of the enormous one
of being the UN of this of enamel poles of that of the zeta drawer of Reimann of gotterdang
of knot burlap then perturbing the priority burlaps
they give conject priority to the carb strip
the selected functor of which could jeopardize
the distribution of primes.

L 'off objective I control from
the case that you have convergence on the zeta strip
of the expert in the von neumann architecture of time
of the parent NP of fixed parameters of convergence
of fast fourier populations carrying one disturbing rule of jump
that supposes the enormous spatial search of its glassa over this
over the poles of Chebychev fitting the periods to the number of parents
orientated 10 NP to the number of their announcements
to the zilog of the elliptical integral of the second kind
of the population collocation to the UN of Seth
a convergence more than the convergence of the fast one
more than the blob flying Lott over the sea of Torrance
more than the retarded argument of the delay
more than the unilateral withdrawl from stolen land.

According to esterno
the equation of the difference of the recurrent give step
differentiates the objective of the walker
from the jive polynomial given ascent in the eastern hole of the feasible give tube
give min give by give rim
give me the risk of maximum return
give k paragrafi to the ones who safeguard the long walk
give the gift of annealing disorder to the destiny of acquaintance of the problem of on
give relax give simulate give misconvergence
give the cody choso
the quartic Foxholes of the shekel
give it give della give quarto the one spectral radius of the Cofrog
the worked on problem on the ouskirts of Cofrog
give hill give down give be give capture
of the always random walk.

This question is naturally of interest
to the table makers at the root of burn
a throw back to the reign of turbulent seeing
off gassing this question of tables
going burn going roxy going attenuation going beautiful of the long ball
going star market for the little eggs in the three pack
going chunks for the young guys
going boing going bebe
related to the ever looping phase shift of the reciprocal of the hyperbolic cosine
the gaussian schmear of the pili wrap
xoring wesley's cyclic dispersion down the fiber optic tube of total internal reflection
erbium doping page by page
I'm wearing the kahukus of soliton
with the looper of these pulses
going solo.

You short on synchronous sin port
you payload of tributary photonic of the sub-layer
you cobject assumption of the collision pipelineing the NAK of blicking aperatures
very small bites filling the fires of NAK
blocked on the process of the distance of hamming
in the assumption of the collision of the multiplex
in the single channel of the will
in the nonsense of the carrier
in the binary exponential backoff of the station
hidden in the backoff the reflectometry of the problem
of the station of slotted aloha and the busybodies
the love I feel for this characteristic
that crosses the double secret account of coax
eating the brekkies of time for the halting of coax
a tree to cut the parity of the horizon
in order to solve the problem of crimping
the vampire tap obtained from the neighbors.

Of clobbering of stopped choking
of the reception of the neighbor
of the flooding of mile
of possessing the token with of
the annendation of the promiscuous fork of that
the corromp of verification and the sum of the frame
being the horizon of left cuts of what paragraphs of hat
of the elasticity of curves to the un of listen
of the elasticity of the auditron of packet of circuit
the un the un the disposition of Linus
the un the un of that of it given she of infinite UN of branch
of outside of employee of in the house of pain
the un the un explaining a bursty traforo
in giving bursty I of the dell of they of those who transmit
the dell of therefore of that one
that I obstructing shiny silicon
of trying the being of silicone
in the dell of hacks
in the courts of misinformation
in the cell rate you so proudly affirm the glory
of my generation.

The nothing is declaring for spiegarlo
who's given to nothing the elasticity of hats
the crowning of spiegarlo for nothing
of having the low one look inside the doggie maw of kerberos
into the expert of the elasticity of the nail of task
task of the thing the power of we
trading for the expert the power of I
for a handle I have a descriptor
for the price of the paragraphs that control it
reezing to negotiate the unethical behavior
molto to shut up of dell the approximated he of timing
the etc example of paragraphs
the one great difficulty of this one of paragraphs
of having of I of the word of best of the spiacente to satisfy
a work under the new of the radical
within the change of the social
believing to create the beautiful model.

To refer to created of the geometry
or paragraph of paragraphs of the exists
of the metasurface of the one of meatballs
of those of the force of one where is the new class
at the meeting of the decoder of the setitimer
the getitimer of poly gonebye
that p of the geometry of IF
if there are created from the carves of the nurb the monifer of CAD
if sharpshooting they give to the interchange of data the polymorphic reconstruction of persistent objects
of time of slashify
manipulating the widgets of Hilandero of string toll
the creator of the carves of the nurb
the cobject monifer of sharpshooting CAD.

Rebajora to Ruby Haskell
statement factory to turn final spectacular
this is the interrupting is
or is the encaminiamento
this of the vector to another one of crankback
or the rechaziamento of the possible world
or with the end of the circuits the earthing of must
or IF the apparatus of Ott
or IF the filatore to be
not the one hard canned in the immediate
nor the ruling of the spin lock
can turn enclosure to the uplane of that
or the mux of inver illustrates the silence of the concept is khaki
which is what collection of points
or what hull can deadlock the requested one
or one creatina of that.

Começ of fa socket
of that of the case of Only fa
hand of one of address of memory its fa estaçion
fa is the data of Somone's fa port
number of fas est-ce que gate sin port
of fa of obstrufa
tree and round robin fa
of puncture final valle stack one FAWOULDBLOCK
I fa break to router some fa
I break fa to fafa harem accompanying a group of management fa
flattering astable control blocks of possible faç
careful 048 est-ce que plant spalling of interest
indicaçion of remote object fa fa unicast
il estend of il server of il classroom of il abstract il public static
il cozine della multivibratore fa
il that of di il that of one il cred
Che il one of il inside of
to blackadder and of arp.

Preprocessing the system of romp
of ifndef of operation
from the archives of no consent
of no process of no index
of no device is defective
of no child of no number of the archives deflective of error
not allowed richium of the memory of the process of prov
of format along too much arg list
of richium of device of the complex roots of unity
the tube of connection of too much system of the archives
of no liabilities in terms of the illegal one
of the device of no space left
of large of too much of the occupied archives
of the archives of too much of the machine
the archives not the UN of April of Tobbac
a valid index of being the UN of index
the not story of no UN of connection
the not functional one field
of the sonic youth.

When the Pathogenic Wind Comes

You of broken consecution
put verwelk the wire so that access through a manhole is possible
met and gone your extrêmes are incited
lightning segments desheathed of the wire must its heat insulation
matrix in two the one linked sgement to be divided
matrix in two that becomes one switch housing
that of a consecution of segments has met access points
of more manner switches along van
Van which of that the man breach it is
it where consecution of broken is cover
man breach cover within can confirm the ING problems in consecution
you of It beccomes broken head pain
with panting of the farynx
sharp edema of the limbs remembers one half proximaal jet of van
to the styloid process of the radius
to the ode of the obstructed river
1.5 cune above the cross sectoral fold of the pulse
in a small cavity of mrs isringhausen
the beam of an air lamp settles in yin valley
in the log of a regular state of an open lunger
cannalvan of binding kicks luo of trapbestelwage
de that of the van that of the lung canalvan of English

meeting the combinations the conceptineschip illustrative met creek
of pain for yangxi met English trigger finger
met that lightning storms can clear the sky
lower fires integrity and higher integrity feels
a burning sensation in the hand
of broken sequence.

Over here shenmen
is the inner one of Of
with the posterior one of shu
with the hysterical xinshu of the heart
with the point of low fright on the rule of the wrist of ulnare of calm
of Of of Of of of of of aphasia of asthma
of Of of of of of in case of the pain of Of
of qi palpitations and the nebulizer
of the heart forthwith dazhong
with second space and the flange of of for arrythmia
of cardiac for desire of the large one
vaporizing more than want more than disinterest
with second space and the splice of the junction
of sleeping in order Of small rabbet
of the point of connection for clearing excessive of of of
of the uterino of the rabbet for reckless movement of blood
of the heart of intestine with its inability to eat here
linguetta expressionless fright
of the divergent channel of it is the germoliturgia ahead of the heart and of when
of it is here of the excess heaviness of of
of it is the four limbs and the head
devoid of the one unexpected of loss of voice

according to the ode the tongue is the sprout of the heart
according to the pivot I dredge the jade of make
of it provokes the inner UN of excessive thought of that
the heart and the apprehension of lesions provoke loss
the heart of loss provokes fright
the heart of fright penetrates the interior.

At the intermediate aspect of the foot
one cune earlier headroom behind the large toe
large by combination of the family name adjusts yellow stomach
large by loosening the humidity harmonized in the middle jiao
palrako stomache average fever pain
which vomits the struation seingeweidehard
into the perforated bucket of aflojandó
by binding more from missed malasadas at the contributing channel of point
the one diverse channel of ying lacked bucket
the spleen is the ruler of the blood
the empanadas of the Maniesorge of feet
as a pain of the drums of paragraph heats itself with the borborygmus of plants
by perforating the ship it missed raises
epilepsy in accordance with the prevented river
climbs down is yin is often at grandfather
grandchild is contributing to the middle jiao
by adjusting the ship so that aflojandó can treat the chest
during the season of spleen in accordance with the prevented river
with THE FINGER of the great one and the hot feet of eat
with the combinations behind cradles of the internal one of separation
in jiao of means ancestor child.

In connection with the canaletas
since a canaleta will call join
of it it is main of connecting
of the narrow channels of the ones it is principal
with the prelude the canaleta installed the prelude made yin
the liver opens to the eye
and makes fire above the divergent one of AA
it makes IQ of scatter
makes the liver cancel bodisattva
gall cannaletas make the malleolus médiale
make the posterior one of the margin close to the gutter of the ankle
a heat sign of moisture makes low more of jiao
a regular pain makes testicles that inflated
one suffered a difficult priapic fact
fact the globus hystericus made in connection with war
a reverse of the subparagraphs of curve and spring
a canaleta divergent makes gall an erection in the ceaseless springtime of levantar
can anybody made when adolesence
a gasoline is liver abundant and of returns
to be it can of the abnormal case pathological be widened
to be it can govern the sinews
while you ignite your indica

pathological subparagraphs of a condition
of oppression of concern and the ships in the field
of throat as when blocked by one plum pit
the stringer of the flow and the menses
with crooked spring and great pouring
clear stasis in woodworm canal.

Large K-4 of dazhong
of kidney van Bell
large is when where behind of this the knees médiale do fork
tendon canaleta calcaneous connection to the point of the leg calcaneous enter
of asthma of kidney do
are the malaria of the prisoner of neurasthenia of hysteria of soreness pharynges
pain do absolutely no jump
qi of chevalement in the lumbar region of stiffness
strengthens want and dispels languette of the dryness of the defermer
desire remain for fear of the door and absolutely no rest
when the master of limn is the lung
and the carrot of limn is the kidney
when only an agreement of this in breathing
is in communication for evacuation
of dyspnoea when none additional of lung
under the inadequacy of AA and above the excess of this of
as the consultation of the circumstance healthily doses both of these
an inadequacy of shaoyin lets fear of the foot take the inadequacy of blame
of the somnolence of subparagraphs of important command points
of him does link kidney by canaleta
luo does levanta of kidney
does dazhong and ascends lumbar strike
on the gong show of great bell.

Dipped jiuwei telegraphs it
from cable number one it is a ship of the conception in the harbour
it points at the summer monitoring function of luo
located seven cune directly above the navel
first of all dived cable
cable dove immediately to the outer dessus of the navel
which seizes angina under a xiphoid process of flaring
one cune of the 7 santa anas of otto
part of one half one cune of hixup
asthma adjusts the heart positions the procedure and the peace suit
which form drawers from legos and crates
porting the case of sumashedhiny nivine
pour it to mature persons of noise from at speaking dislike
pour the violent and that Palpation of fear
the painful pour which taps to bring cables out of throats
pour exaggerated the envoy is more swept than the plains of saskatchewan
more sea ranch than the last nite of summer camp
more cheese board than the sexual activity of the yutes
therefore ceux qi of exhaustion
of telegraphs on the outer dessus of spreading
the dipped wing of proportional form to proportional form
veins of the kind of procedure reflect its xiphoid process

that from the EEC of it and the cases of in ceux qi
while wheezing the illness of the above mentioned if
will kashley and dispnoeo go in gao of it threads
in order to treat with difficulty
the stems and joints of a double-secret
double-lapped dove tail.

21 dabao are fogging it
of it is hence an expert in developer
of the cannal of the large dependent envelope of piglet
who typically pays the spleen from the drains of the continental shelf
the envelope of piglet is all holes for fifteen software
in particular the rule of the nineteenth hole for the fog of eastie spleen
to command the blood the moog of drains is tapping the dead zones of functional analysis
in a yin of appareillé we are given a lower education
of cannal wires of yang of a primary cannal
its leads to link the pay of two with the sickness of the destitute
where bug is your reward
to pay that regulate mediator of neuralgia one hundred axilla of joints
of six cune anterior to au dessous
au dessous a line of one thousand coupled cannals
on average the mediator of midbrane of space of an asthma
in particular an axe predicts badly given a substantial risk of neumothorax
they of costale of area enjoy and unbind the travelling box
known largely by its fog of ash dabao
the travelling box in a vulgarising three emerges from the westernmost hillock of thrace
three cune north and three costale of area
there in pain is the body
flasque of the one hundred joints amounted to or of an embrace of cannal

with axis the pin of heaven and bobo the pin of ground
upper area licks big envelope.

Avant soutiens gorge on surplus transfers
from on cune river to the valley of the three transitions
before cootchie takes a new line on épistaxis
of the recent bride palsey and the almond inflammation of boars
while gorging on the ouvant Neuralgia of before
while you have tinnitis
away drives the wind and the release of heat
and opens those from the transitions of water
which transfer the large point of the EEC to luo
to the joint of entrails more from the connection at kiefer
adjusting the entrails of the crosspiece at the nose of luo
perforating the connection of the eye at stomach
opening the symptom and water the transfer point
it from itself to adjust it consistently to fall on same stage of symptom
treating the edema of asscites and the borborygmus of shoes
my tinnitus that fists the connection of OS
the transferring hiny greating them nosebleed
I-6 of that to affect from them to it to go it from mower
the transition with rinitti pali
which transfers yang from the river of surplus to the chan ho park of lawn
to the lead off walk of the front lawn
watering opens from passage to the stencil of the adjusted clearing

from heat the stencil wind for passage
from the intestine of this joint it rises from ears of slip to angle to kiefer
of crosspiece of sufficient large during the concoction
of joints of stencil of trough of too much stomach before nose
between positionate matter are perforated them
which transfers from the point that too often from itself opens to nans ZuZu
to transfer one tinnito of combines
to go épistaxis on the bank of the versantesi
of veering passage.

Why pain eliminates the state
and the joint values reached
it facilitates the heat of the outside and diminishes the luminous beam of Ulna
on the posterior surface of the wrist two cune from the styloid process
of General External Barrier to Cold
of the fever and the evils of head
it represses the inner one and blocks on a batch of top wind
when the yang linking vessel is diseased
mumps beyond the point confluent
lacrimation of the collar triples in a run
off the pericardium the burner and the joints
the luo point fills a vase of the colleague
over the point of the reunification of hessia
outside the barrier a vase that is often the colleague
outside the barrier a difficulty with the second classic
mud that attacks the sixth tie of the public schema
cubes the song for wind
the humid ones is here outside the pathogenum
oof the summer heat and the head chill and the outside barriers that use jade hits
of the classic excavatrice for the relations of saint jiao
who belongs to a relative of fire and the golden medicine of the mirror
of moxibustion in compliance with the methods of the three jiao

they connect the silicone outside the heat barrier of clinical practice
of the inside gun of the origin of joints
of the posterior part of the macatura of the model
too much irradiates the silicone
the pain is outer gate.

They understand this agency noon is extreme
incapable qu' it also joins the pulsation
contributing and pushing what governs and all it requests
it the liver governs uprising
of poking the tail for mad singing and walking
and aversion to people talking
and triple riscaldore of carried out of is
attitude to them l' calmly
of mentioned of figure of peak hours to a point at the tip of ting
of fous to walk around on all fours doing this
the tend or aiguëment of l'being
a repression is possible at the border of s
repression for concerning the stray horn of simply east
to walk around fou and go on speaking of dell'
to the easiness if he is ready to l' dawn
a figure of peak hours to a point on the three entities of piedino
of is possible of l'doing
of being thoroughly of tend or accutely
of groups to melt of must of that
of your point of source and miens
the melt declared must ying its they under behar
of points for bodies in heat dell'

dicton are song of d'agitate of disorder of dell'
for exaggerated concern of overthinking to present
insurrection of gouverne of liver dell'
they are of breaches of saumure of dap to challenge
of riductions of skinflints and functie-oriënteren
of model dell UNO of develops
of seriously of "chi"
d'fright boosted of that d'still adequate of chimiquex
of products of lack of you does not believe for each of l'round-offs
of gasters to move of soubassement nell' boosted
are ready of all if of the facility of of if in
of and leave of go you'd'in
action of things of assignment
understood the paddle of amounts of that
of word of transmits of then start.

Change d'a No dell' treatment
of UN had feet from 10 of l'art-art
of the ray of inches of 0.1 of nail dell'
0.1-inch from the Department
for larry reynaud the main question is vasodilation
the triple heater of distribution indicates groups
divided in groups of position of debt of deficiency and false cold
of the dewey point of 10 member-members
level with the lower border of the symphysis pubis
in a depression with thigh flexed lateral to the sartorius muscle
surging qi is a point on the pentrating vessel
hidden white can move stagnation in the body in general
needles of after can actively move the complete and the dell' in general
po an era of liability of movement in general
painful persisto has it moving by the points of bluastro black of sbiadiamento
with the opening point of the thoroughfare channel
with earth's crux especially in the lower abdomen and legs
with six pericardium and toes
with inner pass and the notice
with sea of qi l'being beforehand continued of anchors
successively announcing moreover that this blockage can occur
that the left face is warm

that the pinky notches the color of the new piedini
of while using of was neat again
of it can generally be of body dispersing
of it reinforcing and faces the thigh of of
with midnight bulbs it motions the sinfisi superiolateral of of of
more than the manly pubis of edge dell'
more than midnight bear tongue is four spleen opening there
more than the main function of stomach heat with raving is to move side saddle with the
muscle of sartorius
it has thigh of the imbroglio of compression
it has stream divide of rushing yang
it has three leg mile of Compartment.

To the good folks of the Subpoetics, Subpress and Flarf email groups.

To Stephanie Young for including portions of Some Math in the Bay Poetics Anthology.

To the Small Press Traffic Poet's Theater for the opportunity to perform the mass poems accompanied by a video presentation of baseball bloopers edited by Konrad Steiner and inspired by David Buuck and Michael Nicoloff.

To Delraycross at Shampoo for publishing math and acupuncture poems.

To Kevin Killian and Dody Bellamy for printing some of these poems in Mirage and letting me come to the writing class.

To Lyn Hejinian and Olivia Clare for printing the filesystem poems in Ghosting Atoms.

To Lauren Levine, Catherine Meng, and Jared Stanley at MRS Maybe for publishing some of the acupuncture poems.

To Kasey Mohammed and Anne Boyer of Abraham Lincoln for publishing Allystre Julian Certified Orient Minimal Clothing.

And no doubt I've left some names out. Sorry about that. This book has been cooking for over 10 years and my memory is not what it once was. Thanks. Scott.

Acks

Thanks to everyone who invited me to read this work and who helped me along critically. Bard, The Poetry Project, New Yipes, The Bowery Poetry Club, Cannessa Gallery, The University of Maine, The Boston Poetry Marathon, The Bay Area Poetry Marathon, The University of California, Subtext, KSW, Zinc Bar, Small Press Traffic, The Poetic Research Bureau, Artifact, The Scourge of the House Reading, etc. Hi. I love you.

Juliana Sphar, Charles Weigl, Doulgas Rothschild, David Larsen, David Buuck, Lisa Jarnot, Sianne Ngai, Dan Farrell, Peter Culley, Alli Warren and Brandon Brown have provided love, support and critique. Steve Evans and Jennifer Moxley love Don't Stop Believing by Journey.

Steven Matheson and Jenny Lion have take me many places that do show up in the poems. I hope you notice those moments!

Lytle Shaw printed a portion of Some Math and invited me to perform the work at the Drawing Center in New York City.

The Print Center in New York City fashioned a letterpress broadside on the occasion of a reading of Some Math.

Thanks to Bhanu Kapil for healing hands and hosting some of the acupuncture poems in Taurpalin Sky and thanks to Christian Peet.

Thanks to Patrick Durgin for doing a small imprint of Some Math and this larger exposition.

To Geoff Young at the Figures for publishing Swoon Rocket which is interspersed throughout.

To the Kootenay School of Writing (KSW) for printing Some Math in their journal and granting me a phd for $100 US.

Also from Kenning Editions

Ambient Parking Lot, by Pamela Lu
PROSE/FICTION ISBN: 978-0-9767364-3-1 $14.95

Hannah Weiner's Open House, edited and with an introduction by Patrick F. Durgin
POETRY/ART/PERFORMANCE ISBN: 978-0-9767364-1-7 $14.95

Insomnia and the Aunt, by Tan Lin
PROSE/MEMOIR ISBN: 978-0-9767364-7-9 $10.00

The Kenning Anthology of Poets Theater: 1945–1985, edited by Kevin Killian and David Brazil
POETRY/DRAMA/PERFORMANCE ISBN: 978-0-9767364-5-5 $25.95

Left Having, by Jesse Seldess
POETRY ISBN: 978-0-9767364-8-6 $14.95

The Pink, by Kyle Schlesinger
POETRY ISBN: 978-0-9767364-4-8 $7.50

sexoPUROsexoVELOZ and Septiembre, by Dolores Dorantes, translated by Jen Hofer
POETRY ISBN: 978-0-9767364-2-4 $14.95 (copublished with Counterpath Press)

Who Opens, by Jesse Seldess
POETRY ISBN: 978-0-9767364-0-0 $12.95